MW01038336

Deliver Me From...

Deliverance for Our Times

by Dr. I. Franklin Perkins

To Hope Yates
God Bless You!
Appreciate
Dr. [signature]
4/21/17

dpRochelle

PO Box 9523
Hampton, Virginia 23670
1 (757) 825-0030
ItsmeDrIFP.org

© 2014 Dr. I. Franklin Perkins. All Rights Reserved

No part of this book may be reproduced, stored in a retrieval system, or transmitted by any means without the written permission of the author.

Second published by dpRochelle 11/29/14

ISBN: 978-0-9862389-1-8

Printed in the United States of America, Hampton, Virginia

Dedication

* * * * *

Dedicated to the memory of

Dwaine E. Fountain, Sr.

who was always there to support my endeavors.

"You Are Missed."

* * * * *

Foreword

Praises to God for the enlightenment to and through a Christian life as generated by this 2nd edition of *Deliver Me From* . . . . Dr. I. Franklin Perkins has categorically enhanced the substance and contents of this masterpiece. Whether or not one has perused the first publication, this sequel will generate and/or enhance a vivacious enthusiasm for Christ. Having the tool and opportunity to read and apply the biblical temperament of deliverance to one's life is the ultimate resolve to every situation.

Dr. IFP has once again provided an escort through the Scriptures to directly impact life-changing results. She takes her responsibility seriously to share God's Word in realistic ways so that once the information is revealed, the line of attack is clear, and one is informed how to be delivered from. . . . Ezekiel 3:19-21 states: "But if you warn a wicked person and he does not turn from his wickedness or his wicked way, he will die for his iniquity, but you will have saved your life. Now if a righteous person turns from his righteousness and practices iniquity, and I put a stumbling block in front of him, he will die. If you did not warn him he will die because of his sin and the righteous acts he did will not be remembered. Yet I will hold you responsible for his blood. But if you warn the righteous person that he should not sin and he does not sin, he will indeed live because he listened to your warning, and you will have saved your life " (HCSB).

Life on this side of the grave is worth living with Christ at every turn of 360 degrees. The decision to live for Him affords one the opportunity to share with others as Dr. IFP has done taking us to deeper depths. With salvation being free, why would one not want to be delivered from . . .? Be Blessed and Be Delivered!!!

Submitted by

Rev. Dr. Arnita Snead Brooks
Visionary & Senior Pastor
Divine Revelation Ministries, Inc.
Virginia

Acknowledgments

Thanks to my husband,

Pastor Derrick, Sr., my son, Derrick, Jr. and my daughter,

Aegious for being there all the time.

Thanks

Rev. Roger Robbins

Many thanks to:

Tamara Williams

"You are really a smart lady."
I appreciate all of your assistance.

Introduction

Occasionally, you may find a book that encourages you to stay strong, as it may seem to build a temporary fortress between you and your troubles. This book will not only convince you to continue to press on, but it will also make you aware of the strongholds that Satan uses to keep you in bondage. It will offer a solution as to how you can choose to be free from the grips of your shortcomings. As you read, be reminded that Christ has liberated you through Calvary's experience and you should no longer be entangled again with the yoke of bondage, *(Galatians 5:1)*. It is because of this liberation that you have authority over every situation that comes your way.

This book is designed to assist you when you find that deliverance is necessary. It is not considered to be exhaustive nor the only road to salvation or deliverance, however, it has much substance and contextual Scriptures that will cause one to do a self-assessment. It will illuminate your way to ultimate freedom if you desire to be honest with yourself.

There are actual stories included in this book that will identify with many who will read them. Those who had these experiences had believed that their stories would help others find his or her independence from the personal prison that holds them captive. The contents of this book will invigorate Christians as they continue to find deliverance through the Word of God. I expect that the Holy Spirit will lead sinners to Christ through the conviction of their hearts. My further anticipation is that the Spirit of God will prompt all readers to seek deliverance from any stronghold that may hinder their Christian progress.

As you examine the chapters in this second edition, let the Lord speak to you concerning whatever your immediate situation may be. Please do not take the negative stance that these experiences did not happen or that this information is overkill, trust that it is biblically sound and has an impact on your spiritual growth. Once you have recognized the need for deliverance, the next step is to make the information applicable to your life as you strive to be *Delivered From. . . .*

Contents

Part I

Deliver Me From . . .

Part II

How Can I Receive . . .

Deliver

Me

From...

Chapter 1

Pride

Focus Scripture:
"Before destruction the heart of a man is haughty, And before honor is humility." (Proverbs 18:12)

Our society has made gods out of those who have great riches and power. Some would even bow down to those who are in positions of authority to please their superior, but woe unto the one that accepts the glory that only belongs to God.

In *Acts 12:21-23,* Herod's pride caused him to take glory for himself instead of offering it to God. He sat upon his throne in costly array, and made a speech to the people of his kingdom. The people gave thunderous shouts of praise to Herod as they declared that his voice was not that of a man but of a god. Herod allowed the people to make him equal with God rather than rebuking the praise that they offered unto him. He enjoyed all of the honors and applause that he received, without properly acknowledging the true and living God, which cost him his very life. God did not permit Herod to remain in his high seat of authority, when he took the glory that was only due to Him. All glory and honor belongs to God Almighty.

How can we tell if someone needs deliverance from pride? Listed below are a few ways to identify those who are full of pride.

1. **People Who Focus Only On Themselves**
For you have said in your heart: 'I will ascend into heaven, I will exalt my throne above the stars of God; I will also sit on the mount of the congregation On the farthest sides of the north; I will ascend above the heights of the clouds, I will be like the Most High.' (Isaiah 14:13-14)

This is what I call the "all about me disease" because "I" is in the middle of pride. Satan is the best example to show why pride is detrimental. This Scripture describes how Lucifer was evicted from his place of high standing. He allowed pride to enter his heart as he attempted to overthrow The Most High God. In the above Scripture, Satan emphatically stated the five "I wills" that led to his demise. He wanted God and all others to worship him as he sat on the mount of the congregation, not just anywhere on the mount, but on the farthest sides of the north.

What would cause Satan to believe that he was capable of overthrowing heaven? Let us take a look at his reasoning. *Ezekiel 28:11-19* refers to Satan's wisdom and perfect beauty. The text expounds on the places where he had been and how beautiful God had created him. He was gifted in the area of music, as he was created with internal pipes.

4

Satan's heart became proud because of his splendor, beauty and wisdom. He became his own horn tooter and iniquity was found in him. He was not satisfied with the position that God had given him. He wanted heaven to be his own. He desired to be God and would stop at nothing to make his desire a reality. Even though he was not able to cast God down from His throne, he was persuasive enough to capture the hearts of at least two-thirds of the angelic population to go along with his diabolical plan. This action, of course, ended his tenure in heaven.

This lesson demonstrates just how important it is for those who focus on themselves to focus their attention toward items of necessity. If they remain caught up with themselves as Satan was with himself, a devastating end is predicted. There is no sin in being beautiful, talented or educated; the sin comes when the beauty, the talent and the education become the center of focus and God is metaphorically put in the trunk of the car.

2. **People Who Keep Contention Stirring Are Scoffers or Scorners**

Cast out the scoffer, and contention will leave; Yes, strife and reproach will cease. (Proverbs 22:10)

Scoffers are found in every church and in the midst of every disturbance. They do not want to be obedient to God nor to anyone who is in authority. They will find ways to cause confusion for the fun of it by throwing rocks and hiding their hands. If they are denied the privilege of having their way or if they are corrected for something that they have said or done, they will cause a major commotion, cutting down anyone who stands in opposition. Scoffers will cause strife and division if they are allowed free course. They will use their negative influence to make "bad apples" out of others. The Bible says that scoffers should be expelled from the population of people, only then will contention come to an end. If they do not receive deliverance quickly, any organization of which they are a part, will suffer massive destruction.

3. **People Who Are Boastful**
They utter speech, and speak insolent things; All the workers of iniquity boast in themselves. (Psalm 94:4)

Those who activate this manifestation of pride are very rude, malicious and intentional with their conversation. They have no respect for anyone nor do they consider the feelings of others. They will say anything to enhance their prideful image. They will boast about their possessions including their material belongings, their level of authority, and their educational accomplishments even if their boasting hurts other people. They may even belittle those who are less fortunate to make themselves look good. Those who are boastful will occasionally use abrupt and abusive language to bring down those who may not agree with them. If they are not delivered, there will be a multiplicity of hurt feelings along the way.

4. People Who Are Arrogant
A proud and haughty man -Scoffer" is his name; He acts with arrogant pride. (Proverbs 21:24)

This Scripture speaks of people who are their own audience. They place themselves in the positions of judge, jury and executioner. They have so much pride that the Bible just named them "Scoffers," *(Chapter 1, Section 2)*, those who act with "arrogant pride". Those who walk in arrogance will exalt themselves to a seat of judgment where they will criticize and condemn others based on their personal opinion. God will not tolerate any self-exaltation, *"The LORD lifts up the humble; He casts the wicked down to the ground," (Psalm 147:6)*.

It is necessary to include an egotistical personality with this title even though it can be added under a few other titles. The best example that describes this type of spirit is often displayed by men although it can also be found in women. However, I will discuss it from the male ego prospective. Ego issues are an extension of pride most often acquired during childhood because of perhaps an overbearing parent, events that portrayed men having the upper hand over woman, physical or sexual abuse. This person has low self-esteem but bully's others to make themselves feel superior all the while feeling scared and like a little person inside. If a woman who is in a position of authority over him, he will try to diminish her by ignoring her position of authority or belittling her because he needs to feel superior to her. He will not accept her as an equal no matter her position, education or financial status. He feels that a woman's place is in the home and not outside the home instructing men what to do. Unfortunately, I have experienced this ignorance and can spot it a mile away. When I am around this spirit, it becomes uneasy and eventually rears its head. I give it to God!

These manifestations of pride are not only dangerous to the people that are hurt by them, but moreover to those who possess them. The demon pride will isolate people from their loved ones and also from others that they may meet; they will find themselves very much alone if they are not delivered.

While I was in a deliverance session with a woman some time ago, she began to manifest some of the characteristics of pride. Her speech became arrogant and boastful and then she began to cry softly after verbalizing her dissatisfaction about life's issues. I asked her why was she crying, and she stated that she felt small on the inside and inferior to others so she hid behind a wall of haughty behavior to keep others from finding out what her weaknesses were. She began to discuss other manifestations of pride that had a stronghold in her life such as perfectionism, vanity, frustration with others, and her need to feel important. After exposing some of the elements of pride, the Lord delivered her from the haughty spirit, *(Proverbs 16:18)*, and she is now delivered today.

Have you allowed pride to rule your life? Do you parade around as a boastful untouchable? You may feel that you are better than others and think that you know it all. You may even believe that you have it all together and do not need the Lord for anything. If so, let me offer a word of advice; learn to give God the glory that is due to Him. Listen more to others and speak less about yourself and your accomplishments; let God exalt you, *"A man's gift makes room for him, And brings him before great men,"* *(Proverbs 18:16)*. Otherwise, you may ultimately face the same fate as Herod. Whether or not we wish to admit it, the world revolves around God, and He will refuse to accept the proud but will bestow His grace on those who are humble before Him, *(James 4:6)*.

Everybody is not designed to be in the forefront. There are some who are in the background that God will exalt in due season, *"Therefore humble yourselves under the mighty hand of God, that He may exalt you in due time,"*

(1 Peter 5:6). God is the only one who deserves glory and honor and if you receive His glory, you are setting yourself up for failure. God sent an angel to smite Herod for stealing His glory, let this be a lesson well learned.

Pray this prayer for deliverance from pride. "Lord, I need Your help to release my pride. I have hurt many people and have acted in ways that did not bring glory to You. I want You to dwell in my heart, as I learn to wear humility. Help me to see that it is not about what I have done, but it is all about You and who You are. I will vow to give all praise to You, as I strive to humble my heart to You. In Jesus' name, Amen."

Chapter 2

Lying

Focus Scripture:

"Deliver my soul, O LORD, from lying lips And from a deceitful tongue. What shall be given to you, Or what shall be done to you, You false tongue?" (Psalm 120:2-3)

A lying spirit is used as a deceitful trick of the devil to persuade us to believe bits and pieces of inaccurate information, which will ultimately cause us to drift further from our relationship with God. I can remember one of my elementary school teachers coaching me on the way to answer a multiple-choice question. She pointed out that if any part of the answer is false, then the whole answer is false. The half-truth answer is disguised to see if you really know your material, or if you can be swayed to another possibility. This is deception. If any part of the answer is false, then the whole answer should be investigated.

These days, lies are believed before the truth will even be discussed. I recall a preacher saying "a lie can get around the world before truth can get up to put on its clothes." Most people would rather someone tell them a lie instead of telling them the truth because of how comfortable it makes them feel, *"You love evil more than good, Lying rather than speaking righteousness,"* *(Psalm 52:3).* It is plain and simple; the truth cannot always be handled but is needed.

Politicians lie to voters to offer a feeling of security; supervisors lie to employees on the job to keep them performing their daily tasks; spouses lie to one another to keep each other from leaving; and Christians lie to one another to keep from offending their brother or sister. It seems that people lie about so many things that truth is no longer expected. This is not the way in which God intended things to be. We should be able to speak the truth in love, at the right time, no matter how difficult it may be to receive.

A lying spirit is dangerous and has caused many churches to split, many homes to be broken, many lives to be lost and many relationships to be severed. A lying spirit should not easily influence us, but there should be enough Word in us to recognize the deception of being steered in the wrong direction. Pay close attention to how the Word of God teaches us to follow the path of truth at all times. We are warned that many shall depart from the faith because of seducing spirits, which are believed to be truth-tellers, and we are further challenged not to believe every spirit, but to try the spirits to know if they are of God, *(1 John 4:1-3).*

There are many manifestations of a lying spirit however, we will only deal with a few familiar symptoms:

1. Sharing Old Wives Fables And Superstitions

But reject profane and old wives' fables, and exercise yourself toward godliness. (1 Timothy 4:7)

There should be no time spent on concocting, believing or sharing fables or old wives' tales. These stories are fairy tales, which are fantasy oriented and not biblical. I am certain that many of us have passed along a few of these fables and superstitions; such as, a pregnant woman marking her baby by the food she eats; if you step on a crack, you will break your mother's back; if you break a mirror you will have seven years of bad luck; stories of the Easter Bunny who lays eggs for Easter (yeah, right); the tooth fairy, who puts money under the pillow of a child who has just lost a tooth; and the all-time favorite, Santa Claus, who is tasked with sliding down every chimney in the world to place gifts under a tree for only those who were nice. We believe that they sound like cute and innocent stories and will not do any harm, but in fact, they are all lies. We should practice speaking what is Godly not fictitious.

2. A Talebearer Who Flatters

He who goes about as a talebearer reveals secrets; Therefore do not associate with one who flatters with his lips. (Proverbs 20:19)

This person is known as a gossip, which tells anything he or she knows, with a twist to it. One can recognize this dangerous person because they always know everything about everything and everything about everybody. When this person tells a tale, they exaggerate the truth to make it more believable just to keep your attention. This person uses insinuations through eye movements and facial expressions to mislead their audience. If anyone has this type of person in their circle, the Bible says to quickly disconnect from the relationship at once. Remember, everyone has to give an account for every idle (worthless) word when standing before God, *(Matthew 12:36)*. Even offering words of flattery that convey artificial praise is equally as damaging, *"A lying tongue hates those who are crushed by it, And a flattering mouth works ruin," (Proverbs 26:28)*. It is best that a word is not spoken if it is not a word of truth. Be mindful of those who desire to tell the story the way they want to tell it, instead of telling the truth without speculation.

3. **Philosophy And Empty Deceit**

> Beware lest anyone cheat you through philosophy and empty deceit, according to the tradition of men, according to the basic principles of the world, and not according to Christ. (Colossians 2:8)

The Bible instructs us to beware of false prophets, who will come to us disguised as sheep, and how we will recognize them by their fruit, *(Matthew 7:15-20)*. This means that false prophets will avoid telling the whole counsel of

God but rather preach their own watered down gospel to lead the gullible multitudes away from Jesus Christ as far as the east is from the west. This person will say that they come in the name of the Lord, but have devious motives to tear down any knowledge of the truth. They intend to hinder a ministry from operating in effective missions. When traditions, laws and philosophical rituals are exalted above the Bible, beware of the person who endorses them. This is the spirit of error at work, (*1 John 4:6*).

Are you guilty of any of these things? If so, do not let another moment go by without confessing this sin to God. The Bible declares, *"...all liars shall have their part in the lake which burns with fire and brimstone, which is the second death,"* (Revelation 21:8). Do not let this be your bed of eternity.

Now that you are aware of the damage that lying can cause, this is your opportunity to be free from it today. Pray this prayer to release a lying spirit. "Lying spirit, in Jesus' holy name, you must go! You are no longer welcomed in my house. You will not cause any further damage to me. I want the Lord to fill me with His truth and speak through my lips! Lord, I pray that You would seal me, strengthen my heart and continue to dwell here as I serve You. In Jesus' name, Amen."

Chapter 3

Unforgiveness

Focus Scripture:

"But if you do not forgive, neither will your Father in heaven forgive your trespasses." (Mark 11:26)

Holding on to unforgiveness will block our blessings, inhibit our healing, and hinder our spiritual growth. Satan will tell us that it is alright to hold on to unforgiveness because no one else knows that it is there. This act will prevent us from enjoying the fullness of life that was promised to us by Jesus Christ himself, *"The thief does not come except to steal, and to kill, and to destroy. I have come that they may have life, and that they may have it more abundantly," (John 10:10).*

Many of us continue to hold unforgiveness in our hearts because of what someone has said or done to us. The distressing thing, in many instances, is that the person you will not forgive is dead or the incident may have happened several years ago, almost so long ago that the people involved have forgotten just what the offense was. God does not tolerate unforgiveness.

17

I know we may say that others are not worthy of our forgiveness because they really hurt our feelings, but are we worthy of God's forgiveness? No, we are not worthy either, but God still loves us anyway. Jesus Christ displayed His love, by dying on the cross, while we were still sinners. That very act of love justifies us for all eternity, so that we can escape God's wrath, *(Romans 5:7-9)*. So why not forgive? When we do not forgive others and hold a grudge, we are equal to the one who wronged us? Now, let that sink in for a moment.

The focus Scripture states that forgiveness of others is a requirement in order to have our prayers answered. We will not get around the prerequisite of forgiving our brothers and sisters and then think that we can ask God to answer all of our prayers. It is not going to happen! Either we forgive others or stop expecting our prayers to be answered.

If unforgiveness is prolonged, it can turn into hatred toward the individual and ultimately to bitterness because it is held inside for so long. When bitterness is held inside against others, the very mentioning of the offenders name may cause you some discomfort. The root of bitterness can cause us to possess ill thoughts of harm toward the person who has wronged us.

We may sometimes use profane language when referring to them. Sometimes we may refer to them by using animal names or other ugly analogies of what we can imagine. These are tale tell signs that we have not yet forgiven the individual. Sometimes we wish they were dead thinking that our lives would be better off without them in the world. Unfortunately, their demise does not release us from the growing cancer of unforgiveness that we carry around.

We should never feel the need to get back at them; let God handle the matter. He can repay the evildoer far better than we can, *"Beloved, do not avenge yourselves, but rather give place to wrath; for it is written, "Vengeance is Mine, I will repay," says the Lord," (Romans 12:19).*

I can remember some years ago, I had grown bitter with a young lady because I did not want to forgive her for hurting me. For years, I walked around praising God with my lips but holding unforgiveness in my heart towards her. Whenever I saw this young lady, my stomach turned as if I had to throw up. I could not stand to be in her presence. As time progressed, I realized just how much I hated her. I became tense and started having frequent migraine headaches and my stomach would ball in knots. I was having a hard time sleeping at night because I would periodically mull over the wrong that I had suffered. My health was literally falling apart. Over a period of time, things grew much worse, and I began to imagine what my life would be like if she did not exist. Basically, I wanted her dead (yes) and out of my way for good!

One day I saw her praying and this made me feel rather uncomfortable. It was at that moment that the Spirit of the Lord convicted me of the unforgiveness I was holding against her and compelled me to ask her to forgive me for holding a grudge. When I had that conversation with God, my life was turned completely around, and I asked His forgiveness and I also asked the young lady whom I hated to forgive me as well. Needless to say, the migraine headaches stopped, I felt so much better on the inside, I could then sleep at night, and most of all......I was delivered!

One of the most touching letters that I have received concerning forgiveness was from a teenager who attended a service in which I was ministering. This is an excerpt from her letter:

"I was truly blessed by your powerful message that you gave on salvation, while you worshipped at my church. It opened my eyes to how I needed to change my ways and forgive my father for the pain that he has caused me. Through your prayers for me, I have been able to receive my blessings and also help others with the Word from God that you gave. I fully understand now and I am focused on GOD. Please keep me in

your prayers. Thank you again and may God continue to bless you." I praise God for the results!

If you have been hurt by someone, pray and ask God to help you get over the hurt, and bear in mind, if you continue to live, you will probably be hurt again. *Psalm 37:1* says not to fret over evildoers or the iniquities that they work, because sooner or later He will cut them off. It may seem that they have the upper hand now, but by and by their time will run out. Keep your mind focused on those things that are pure and holy and avoid rehearsing evil thoughts of the past. Wait patiently on the Lord, and He will handle the matter in His time.

Whatever you do, please rid yourself of the disease unforgiveness. The end result is devastating and life is too short to hold a grudge. Do not let anyone's external actions dictate what your internal response will be. Let it go!

Now that you are aware of the damage unforgiveness can cause, this is your opportunity to be free from it today. Pray this prayer for unforgiveness to leave. "Unforgiveness, in Jesus' name, you must go! You are no longer welcomed in my house. You will not cause any further damage to me. As you go, take all other evil spirits associated with you and do not return to my house. Lord, I ask that You would forgive me and fill my heart with love and forgiveness. Please strengthen and seal me as I serve You. I ask that You help me forgive

_____ (insert each person's name) for the harm that they have caused me. In Jesus' name I pray, Amen."

Chapter 4

Not Trusting God

Focus Scripture:

"Trust in the Lord with all your heart, And lean not on your own understanding; In all your ways acknowledge Him, And He shall direct your paths." (Proverbs 3:5-6)

What do you do, when you do not know what to do? Has there ever been a time in your life when you could not turn to the left or to the right for direction? Have you ever felt as though you were trapped in a box with no way out? Have you ever prayed to God, while going through a crisis, and it seemed as though He was neither available nor compassionate toward your frustrations? Just trust God!

I am sure you have heard the saying "the darkest hour is just before day," even though it may seem that your day may never come. As a matter of fact, you may be in a midnight crisis as you are reading this book, but there is a solution to your problem. Let us see how trusting God has helped others in their darkest hour.

1. **Trust In The Lord**

The book of Job tells us of a man who was perfect and upright in the eyes of God and did all he could to please the

Lord. He even acted as a priest for his sons regularly as he offered burnt offerings to God for their sins.

But one day, after the devil had a meeting with God, he told God that he could make Job curse Him to His face if God would allow him to get to Job's things. Then, in rapid succession, all of Job's oxen, donkeys and camels were stolen, his servants were killed, lightning destroyed his 7000 sheep, and all ten of his children were killed at one time; Job never stopped trusting God.

As you read through the story, you will notice that Job, who was noted for his patience, grew impatient as he began to ponder why God would allow so much devastation to occur in his life. However, through his distress, he did everything but curse God as Satan had assumed he would. Job cursed the very day that he was born, but he held true to his trust in God. Even though he did not quite understand why he had to suffer, he trusted in God's design while going through his torments of life, *(Job 13:15)*. He trusted God to deliver him from his state of tribulation.

2. **Lean Not On Your Own Understanding**

Early on in ministry, I attended a service where I had the opportunity to preach and minister to some of the people. The Spirit of God was speaking words of knowledge through me as individuals would come to the altar for their prayer needs. I was listening attentively as the voice of the Holy

Spirit spoke concerning each need, and I would then pray for that specific need. However, there was a teenager who came to the altar for prayer. I begin to minister to him concerning his life and the great future that he had in front of him. I could feel the pain that he was feeling but the Spirit continued to speak life through me for this young man. I left believing that all was well. To my dismay, I was told that the young man committed suicide six to eight months after that service, the young man committed suicide because of the pressure he was facing at school. I was devastated to believe that God gave a word of knowledge concerning his future but did not fulfil it.

After I received this message, I questioned trusting God when I heard another word of knowledge. I was embarrassed and felt as though I delivered a false word. Confused about this incident I asked God what went wrong and did I hear His words correctly? He responded that there was nothing wrong with the word given but it is the responsibility of the individual to receive it and wait on the manifestation. This is when I discovered that we are the only ones who can stop a word of prophecy from coming to pass in our lives. The devil cannot stop it and God will not stop it because it is His word so, we can either get into agreement with God or listen to the other guy. My heart was saddened because he had so much promise.

I asked the Lord to forgive me for not believing that I heard Him correctly and promised that I would never doubt His voice again.

Now, when the Spirit of God gives me a word of knowledge or prophecy to share with someone, I vow to Him that I will always trust His guidance, knowing that He will never lead me in the wrong direction. I will not be deterred nor intimidated, even when people may say that they need prayer for something else; I trust God.

3. **He Will Direct Your Path**

Acts 16 talks about the ministry of Paul as he traveled to share the gospel throughout various cities. He was so excited about the gospel that he wanted to communicate it to everyone. Paul tried to go to parts of Asia to preach the gospel, but was forbidden of the Holy Spirit to go. Instead, He directed Paul's path through a vision of a man pleading with him to come to Macedonia. The Holy Spirit directed Paul's steps where his ministry was most needed.

Sometimes we may find that the places we want to go may not be the places where God wants us to be. It is so important to be guided by the Spirit of God in order to be effective. As He directs our pathway, we should follow His leading with high expectations.

One or all of these stories may assist you when you are going through storms in your life. Try trusting God to see the things that you cannot see, to fix the things that are broken inside and to oil the areas in your spirit that are dry. Please bear in mind that things are not going to be easy everyday of your life, so do not throw in the towel. For God wants us to give Him all of our cares so that He can handle them for us, *"casting all of your care upon Him, for He cares for you," (1 Peter 5:7).* Why not take Him up on this proposition.

Take a moment to read *Psalm 115:12-15*, it will show how God has us on His mind. He wants so desperately to bless our families and us for many generations to come. Just trust God! We are not equipped to do things all on our own. There are times that we may think that we are in control, but that is when things really go haywire. Once we have messed up everything, God will then have to step in to straighten things out for us. He will allow us to get in a jam so that we can humbly remove ourselves from the equation. This humbling experience will teach us how to trust God.

Jeremiah 10:23 reminds us that God orders our steps, *"O LORD, I know the way of man is not in himself; It is not in man who walks to direct his own steps."* God wants us to trust Him as an infant trusts his parents, completely dependent upon them for their needs and desires. The infant does not know if it will have food to eat, a place to stay or clothes to wear yet it eats, has a place to stay and clothes to

27

wear without any concern. If we trust the leadership of God, and acknowledge Him in all of our ways, He promises to grant us direction and to take care of all our need.

The next time you feel like you are trapped, lost or confused, let *Proverbs 3:5-6* sink deep into your spirit to remind you that God knows in which direction He wants you go; follow His leading. Do not trust in others to help you move to the next level, because people will let you down; stop trusting in your book sense, because your knowledge is limited; stop trusting in your money, because it can only take you but so far; stop trusting in horoscopes, tarot cards and good luck charms, because there is no real power there to assist you, simply apply the principle of trusting in God alone.

Pray this prayer for God's direction. "Lord, please forgive me for doubting Your ability to guide me. Help me to trust You as You handle my life's crisis. My vow today is to remove myself from the driver's seat and let You chauffeur me through the traffic of life. I now realize that Your direction will ensure my destination's arrival. In Jesus' name, Amen."

Chapter 5

Fear

"For God has not given us a spirit of fear, but of power and of love and of a sound mind." (2 Timothy 1:7)

Boo!! I hope that did not startle you. You may laugh, but there are those who would jump through hoops and run like the wind when confronted with that three-letter word. Some children are scared to death that monsters are either under their beds or in their closets, and many are afraid of *"the dark."* Not long ago, my nine-year old daughter would run through the house screaming, when by-passing dark rooms; she used that method as a measure of security. Sounds ridiculous, does not it? Well, I have encountered just as many adults who are afraid of some of the same things as children, if not more afraid than children.

In the focus Scripture, Timothy, states that the Lord does not give us the spirit of fear; obviously, this is not one of the attributes of God nor is it in His "top nine" list of the fruit of the Spirit. God does not assign fear to anyone; He offers wonderful gifts of value. So, if the Lord does not impart the spirit of fear, then who else is there to send it our way? There is only one other entity from which this spirit could come

29

............the devil. God offers power, love and a sound mind in lieu of fear; the devil suggests fear. You make the choice.

There are several manifestations of fear, which may be a surprising illumination. Listed below are just a few areas of fear that may affect our daily walk:

1. **Tomorrow's Worry**

Now if God so clothes the grass of the field, which today is, and tomorrow is thrown into the oven, will He not much more clothe you, O you of little faith? Therefore do not worry, saying, 'What shall we eat?' or 'What shall we drink?' or 'What shall we wear?' (Matthew 6:30-31)

Why trouble ourselves with concerns of tomorrow which may never come, or rather, that we may never see arrive? Tomorrow is not promised to anyone. Even if we knew what would take place tomorrow, there is little that we could do about it. We should live for today, because that is all that we have. Having fear of issues and difficulties for tomorrow, will rob us of our joy for today. There is nothing wrong with being prepared for anticipated situations, but let us not become so consumed with its arrival, that we forget God has already lived in tomorrow and is waiting for us to arrive. He knows exactly what we need before we ask for it, (*Matthew 6:32*). Let God continue to hold the future.

2. Fear Of Man

The fear of man brings a snare, But whoever trusts in the LORD shall be safe. (Proverbs 29:25)

Being afraid of what man will say or do, can drive us mad. There is no possible way to keep up with the various temperaments of man without falling into a trap. One day, man may approve of what we are doing and the next day he may disapprove of the same. This fair-weather nature is very hard to please and will cause undue pressure to the one fearing the opinion of man. We should only fear God. For He is the One who can destroy the body and the soul, (*Matthew 10:28*).

3. Heart Failure (Heart Attack)

Men's hearts failing them from fear and the expectation of those things which are coming on the earth, for the powers of the heavens will be shaken. (Luke 21:26)

Near the end times, fear of apprehension of impending destruction will cause heart failure. The issues of the world have many biting their finger nails and suffering from anxiety as they pondering the terror that is expected to happen could cause one's heart to weaken if it is not guarded with the peace of God. "*Be anxious for nothing, but in everything by prayer and supplication, with thanksgiving, let your requests be made known to God; and the peace of God,*

which surpasses all understanding, will guard your hearts
and minds through Christ Jesus." (Philippians 4:6-7)

4. **Fear Of Death**

Inasmuch then as the children have partaken of flesh
and blood, He Himself likewise shared in the same,
that through death He might destroy him who had the
power of death, that is, the devil, and release those
who through fear of death were all their lifetime
subject to bondage. (Hebrews 2:14-15)

Everyone wants to go to heaven but no one wants to
die to get there because we are terrified of dying. If we die in
Christ it is not a bad thing, based on Scripture, we know what
to expect, and where we will ultimately spend eternity. The
devil will try to keep us at odds with God to imply that we
deserve eternal death, and guess what? We do. But Jesus took
a trip down through the belly of the earth, extracted the keys
from death, hell and the grave, *(Revelation 1:18),* and now
has all power in His possession. When we accept Jesus as
Lord of our life, we are given a clear destination of promise.
It is a fact that we all must travel through the doorway of
death when this life is over however it is up to us whether we
want smoking or non-smoking.

Fear is an approach used by the devil to divert our
attention from matters of importance. It also takes away our
ability to function, because we are distracted. How many
times were we supposed to tell others about the plan of

salvation, but found ourselves too afraid because of what they might say or how they would react to our invitation? We have a responsibility, and *2 Timothy 1:7* suggests that, the Lord has given us three ways to overcome fear, and that is through power, love and a sound mind.

Let us take a look at the power that God has given us. In *Luke 10*, Jesus commissioned additional disciples to go into every city to let the people know that the kingdom of God has come unto them, and He instructed them to heal the sick therein. When they returned from their assignment, they reported with joy how even the demons were subject to them through the name of Jesus. This means that we have unrestricted power handed to us on a silver platter; and guess what friends - we are authorized to use it!! How do we know? Because the Bible says that God has given us that power to be used through the Holy Spirit. The same power that raised Jesus from the dead, and healed the blinded eyes and crippled legs, is the same power living on the inside of us waiting to overtake fear.

Now, let me take a moment to mention this tidbit of information; please do not try to use the first component, power without the other two components, love and a sound mind. The Scripture uses all three as a combination to combat fear, not individually. The Holy Spirit must orchestrate this transaction to avoid a disastrous situation.

God has also imparted love to overcome fear. When we accept Jesus into our hearts we will find that there is no room for fear to dwell because, *"There is no fear in love; but perfect love casts out fear, because fear involves torment. But he who fears has not been made perfect in love,"* (1 John 4:18). So, once love has been deposited within, we will be so full of God's love that fear cannot make a home there to torment us any further.

Finally, Timothy further advises that it is God that gives us a sound mind. The Bible promises us that we will be kept in perfect peace, if our mind is focused on God, simply because we trust in Him, *(Isaiah 26:3).* This passage presents itself to say that our mind should be focused on God rather than items of no consequence, such as fear and other frivolous concerns. Many of us could lose our mind if our thoughts are not focused on things that are true, noble, just, pure, lovely and of good report, *(Philippians 4:8).* Having a focused mind is simply having a disciplined mind. We should practice *"casting down arguments and every high thing that exalts itself against the knowledge of God, bringing every thought into captivity to the obedience of Christ,"* (2 Corinthians 10:5). We have all rights to center our attention totally on God.

The devil's job is to plant the seed of fear and then watch it grow. I have heard stories of people wanting to harm other people through the use of mind control, which is witchcraft. The person practicing witchcraft told the victim that they were going to fix the victim, (which means harm is intended) and from that moment on, the victim continued to look over his shoulders expecting something bad to happen. In all actuality, the person practicing witchcraft planted a seed of fear in the victim's mind and then watched it grow. The victim did more harm to themselves, by focusing on the idea that they would be fixed, then the person who was actually planting the seed of fear. You see, fear has a way of formulating our thoughts, therefore we become what we believe, *"For as he thinks in his heart, so is he…,"* *(Proverbs 23:7).* So, if we believe that we are afraid, then no one will be able to convince us of anything different.

There is no need to be fearful because God has given us all that we need to conquer not just fear but all other types of demonic forces that we will encounter. We should utilize our power through love, and this will enable a disciplined sound mind. Fear will then be paralyzed, and it will not be able to penetrate the surface of our spirit to bring us harm.

The Bible declares that the fearful and other offenders will not escape their part in the lake that burns with fire and brimstone, *(Revelation 21:8),* but deliverance is available today from the torment that the fearful will suffer.

If fear is gripping your heart and preventing you from living to your fullest potential, then this is your opportunity to release it right now in the name of Jesus Christ. If you seek the Lord, He will hear you, and He will deliver you from all of your fears, *(Psalm 34:4)*. What do you fear?

Pray this prayer to be delivered from fear. "Lord God, please bring comfort to my spirit and peace to my mind. Fear, you have no more dominion over my thoughts or actions. You must go now! I want the Lord to dwell in my heart and clear all of my doubts. Lord, I ask You to fill me with Your Holy Spirit as I serve You. In Jesus' name, Amen."

Chapter 6

Envy

Focus Scripture:

"For where envy and self-seeking exist, confusion and every evil thing are there." (James 3:16)

Envy is simply a warning sign that something inside needs to be repaired. If envy is allowed to continue, matters will only become worse. Envy has been thought of as being synonymous with jealousy; however, they have separate meanings, but a similar connotation.

Envy is the intensive longing to possess something that someone else has, not the desire to necessarily leave others without, however if left with no other choice, then it is deprivation for others. While jealousy is a strong feeling experienced by someone who perceives that any affection, love or attention, of their loved one should be given to them versus another. Jealousy encompasses a form of envy, but includes a third party and also suggests a feeling of personal entitlement, which does not present itself in envy.

When the Bible speaks of jealousy, it is always included in Scriptures concerning God's jealousy, or the jealousy of a spouse, *(Numbers 5:14-18, 25, 30), (Numbers 25:11), (Deuteronomy 29:20), (Proverbs 6:34), (Song of*

Solomon 8:6), (1 Corinthians 10:22), and (2 Corinthians 11:2). There is no mention of God being an envious God nor is jealousy used in the same terms as envy, which is toward people in general. It only speaks of God's jealousy of man putting other things before Him and the jealousy of a spouse. Now that we have a working definition for envy, we can proceed with our findings on the subject.

When we began to feel envious towards another person because of the things we desire of them, we are basically saying to God that we are not content with the person He has made us to be. We are also suggesting to Him that we are not satisfied with the possessions He has entrusted to us, *"Let your conduct be without covetousness; be content with such things as you have...," (Hebrews 13:5).* We may need to think this Scripture over before moving on.

The working of envy is so detrimental that it could bring about such results as murder. Let us take a look at the twenty-first chapter of *1 Kings*. King Ahab wanted a vineyard that belonged to Naboth, because it was adjoining his palace. The King demanded Naboth to give the vineyard to him, so that he could plant a garden of herbs. He even offered Naboth another vineyard and also made him a monetary proposal because he really wanted what Naboth had. Naboth quickly declined the offers of the King. Naboth informed the King that the vineyard was an inheritance given to him by his fathers and that he was out of order for even asking for it.

So, the King went home feeling rebuked, with his head hung down, refusing to eat any food because Naboth would not give him what he desired. Soon his wife, Jezebel, noticed his somber behavior and questioned him intensively, until he told her his concern. As it were, Jezebel ordered the men in the city to railroad Naboth into a blasphemous ordeal against God and against the King and then had Naboth stoned to death outside of the city.................all because King Ahab desired something that belonged to someone else.

This may seem extreme, but it still happens today. People have allowed envy to build up inside, until ways of hurt and harm against the person who is envied become the order of the day.

Some time ago, I had a Christian sister tell me that she had been envious of me because she felt that I was everything that she wanted to be in life. She further admitted that she desired my talents, my personality, and my possessions. Quite naturally, I knew that something was wrong, because there seemed to have been an invisible wall that continually distanced our relationship, but I did not know to what extent. Although she was extremely difficult to get along with, but I continued to show her love. She finally approached me to ask for my forgiveness and I forgave her. It was then that I had the opportunity to inform her of all of the hard times and disappointments that I had to endure just to get to the place where God wanted me to be. After explaining to her part of my struggles through life's journey, I began to help her identify some of the wonderful attributes and areas in her life that God had blessed her to have.

She soon admitted that she was insecure about a lot of things, and I was just the scapegoat in which to apply her envious venom. We prayed about her insecurities and failures, as she admitted to her inabilities and shortcomings. She asked God's forgiveness, and she is now delivered.

When you feel that envy is about to overtake you, read *1 Corinthians 13* in its entirety to help you regain focus. Surround yourself with people of love versus a group of folks who share the same dysfunctional views concerning envy as you do. The focus Scripture, *James 3:16,* suggests that only destruction can come of envy. Begin to practice serving others, instead of concentrating on what you think you may want from them. Being selfish and self-serving, will only center your thoughts on you and your own desires. Focus on your relationship with Christ through His Word and through loving others. I can bear witness that love will suppress the envy you may feel toward your neighbor, family member, enemy or friend, *"By this all will know that you are My disciples, if you have love for one another," (John 13:35).*

When you show love to all, you will be glad that others are doing well.

Now that you are aware of the damage of envy, you can be free from it today. Pray this prayer for envy to leave. "Envy, in Jesus' holy name, you must go! You are no longer welcomed in my house. You will not cause any further damage to me. I want the Lord to dwell in my heart and place love there so that I can love my sisters and brothers as commanded by the Word of God, and also to esteem them higher than myself! As you leave, take all other evil spirits associated with you and do not return to my house. Lord, strengthen me as I serve You. In Jesus' name, Amen."

Chapter 7

Attacks

Focus Scripture:

"For though we walk in the flesh, we do not war according to the flesh. For the weapons of our warfare are not carnal but mighty in God for pulling down strongholds."
(2 Corinthians 10:3-4)

One thing about working in deliverance ministry is that when we submit our will to God to move forward in this dimension of service, Satan will try to destroy every area of our lives if he is allowed to do so, simply because we have waged war against his kingdom. We will not be exempt from his fiery darts just because we know how to slow him down. He will meddle in our financial affairs, taunt our family members, harass us at our place of employment, and he will even attack our bodies with infirmities.

There should be no mistake in thinking that the devil cares anything about us because he does not. He is not going to take it easy on us if we are old or young, male or female, handicapped, or mute, black or white, rich or poor; he is always coming up with ways to distract us. Every opportunity he is given to seize our joy, he will jump at the chance. If he should find an opened door to enter, he will not miss that golden opportunity. Even though the enemy waits to pounce on us, *"No weapon formed against you shall prosper, And every tongue which rises against you in judgment You shall condemn...," (Isaiah 54:17).* Yes, a weapon will be formed, but it shall not prosper.

It is said that every psychiatrist needs a psychiatrist. Likewise I agree that every deliverance minister needs a deliverance minister. Many years ago, I visited a deliverance team of ministers to experience my own deliverance. I was suffering from an amalgamation of past hurts and other maladies that were getting the best of me; I needed spiritual assistance. After three days of intense prayer and several deliverance sessions, I felt free as a bird in the sky and strong in my spirit. My drive home was full of bliss and delight and I believed that I could handle anything that came my way. I began to thank God for the victory of my deliverance. Well, about three days after my return is when the attack came while I was inside praying. My eyes were opened and I saw a wind (yes, I saw wind) that was shaped like a figure coming towards me and went through my upper torso. Immediately, I felt a cramp in my neck and in the left upper quarter of my back and I felt paralyzed on that side of my body. The pain grew worse when I tried to move. It was then that I realized that I was under demonic attack because not many days before I received freedom from many major issues. This type of attack was new to me and I had never experience this before, so I called the deliverance team and asked for their assistance. They believed it to be a spirit of infirmity that entered my body and I concurred based on the symptoms. They began to pray over the phone and I was in agreement with them as we denounced the power and presence of that spirit. Within minutes, I felt it leave my body abruptly. I thanked God for the authority that He gave me to pray in concert with two others to receive a breakthrough.

Yes, we have the authority over the attacks of the devil when sent in our direction. We must believe by faith. When Jesus sent out the seventy disciples, *Luke 10*, He empowered them with His authority. What a wake-up call to the devil when he sees us walking in our rightful calling as joint-heirs with Jesus Christ. Hallelujah, we are empowered!

This event was an attempt to hinder the progress of one who was committed to do the work of the Lord. I know we may feel vulnerable sometimes to his attacks, and we are, but because we have been washed in the blood of Jesus, we do not have to watch our own back. That is what God does for everyone who serves Him.

You may say that you do not believe in spiritual wars, but there are battles being fought over you continuously just as the devil challenged Michael over Moses' body, *"Yet Michael the archangel, in contending with the devil, when he disputed about the body of Moses, dared not bring against him a reviling accusation, but said, "The Lord rebuke you," (Jude 9)!* You are worth fighting over.

Pray this prayer for protection. "Lord, I ask that You would protect me from spiritual attacks of the devil and his demons, and I also ask that You would keep me aware of any open doors in my spirit. Lord I ask that You would instruct Your angels to keep charge over me in all my ways, even when I cannot see the attack coming. In Jesus' name, Amen."

Chapter 8

Myself

Focus Scripture:

"O wretched man that I am! Who will deliver me from this body of death? I thank God-through Jesus Christ our Lord!"
(Romans 7:24)

I have struggled with writing this chapter for the past few months. As I sit up night after night wrestling with my flesh, I still find it extremely complicated to express exactly why I am having such a difficult time. The irony of struggling with this chapter..........M-Y-S-E-L-F!

Sometimes I cry out, "Oh God, please help me", when I accidentally or willfully slip into temptation because of my fleshly desires. I find that there is no one who can help me, but God. I realize that my worst enemy… is ME. Therefore, it is in our best interest that we come in agreement with God, so we can successfully defeat the opposition.

There are times when I want to blame someone else for my shortcomings, so I will quickly say, "the devil made me do it." But the Lord tells me to stop lying on the devil and read *Galatians 5:19-21*, where flesh is responsible for a plethora of sin. Some days I feel that I have lost the contest against my flesh, but somehow God allows me to continue to preach, teach and sing under His anointing.

For me, there is now a complete understanding concerning the war that apostle Paul was having with himself. As he cried out about his wretchedness, I cannot help but empathize with his plea; I can identify with the agony he felt. The apostle Paul talks about his constant fight with flesh in the seventh chapter of Romans and how he just could not seem to explain why he did what he did when he did it. He groaned continuously as to how the law provided him with the knowledge of what sin was, which caused him to desire the things that he should not. The knowledge of what is right and wrong then became a struggle for him.

Oh, to live in the Garden of Eden where the childlike and carefree atmosphere was the dominating force before the fruit was eaten. There would be no knowledge of what is right or wrong. For when Adam and Eve ate of the tree, the Bible says that their eyes were then opened, *(Genesis 3:7)*. It was at that moment that the revelation of knowledge made them accountable for their actions. As long as they were innocent to the law, there were not any fleshly desires, but the moment they ate of the fruit, their knowledge of right and wrong became a battle.

I struggle with my flesh daily with different circumstances that may arise in my life, but God has made a way of escape for every temptation that I may encounter, *(1 Corinthians 10:12)*. It is further realized, that the war between my flesh and my spirit will continue until I die. So I will either reject my fleshly desires, or I will give in to them; it is all up to me.

The flesh is greedy and wants to eat, while the spirit is hungry and needs to eat. Whichever one is fed the most will be the stronger of the two.

Pray this prayer for self-deliverance. Lord, help me to overcome my daily struggles, for I can do nothing without You. Forgive me for bringing shame to Your name and deliver me from the fleshly ways that do not resemble Christ. Deliver me from the above listed concerns that continuously trouble my soul. Help me to keep my thoughts and heart pure as I press to conquer the desires of my flesh. I want You to dwell in my heart and restore me to my rightful place as Your child. In Jesus' name, Amen.

How

Can

I

Receive...

Chapter 9

Salvation

Focus Scripture:

"That if you confess with your mouth the Lord Jesus and believe in your heart that God has raised Him from the dead, you will be saved." (Romans 10:9)

Salvation is free to all! That is right, free, with no catches or hidden costs. I know that sounds rather suspicious and hard to believe, but it is true.

Some of the people that I have had opportunity to talk with about salvation expressed that they could not understand why God would want to send His son Jesus Christ to die for a world full of sinners? My answer to them, of course, is that this act was a demonstration of His love for us even though we did not deserve it, *"But God demonstrates His own love toward us, in that while we were still sinners, Christ died for us," (Romans 5:8)*. Wow!! This is His unconditional love displayed for a world full of undeserving creatures.

The way to accept salvation may indeed seem as though it is too good to be true, but the fact is, salvation is not hard to obtain at all. It is a free gift from God and all you have to do is receive the gift. You must receive the finished work of the cross and then you will have salvation.

God will forgive you for all of your sins that you have committed before this transformation. He will forgive you no matter how horrible or disgusting your sins may be. Salvation is the doorway to a glorious eternal life. Where will you spend eternity? That is a question that you should ponder right now. If you have to think about whether you are saved or not, chances are, you need to repent of your sins.

I know you may say to yourself that you do not need this salvation that Jesus offers because you do not hurt anyone, you do not drink, party, or swear, you do not run around or gossip, nor do you hate anybody or break the law, but you live a morally good life. (Remember, we are talking about receiving the gift of salvation, not a country club membership). Well, I do have a news flash for you, *"For all have sinned, and come short of the glory of God,"*
(Romans 3:23KJV). So you see, everyone has done something that was not pleasing in God's eyesight.

Some people believe that since they have been in church all of their lives that they have received salvation through the good works that they have done. Salvation is not predicated on how many good services that are offered to the church or to the community, but it is predicated on the acceptance of the finished work that Jesus did on Calvary's cross over 2000 years ago. No one is saved because of the assistance they offer, nor by doing church work, community

54

services or even through philanthropies; these works should be done because salvation has been received. That is when the ultimate best can be offered to God and others.

If you are not saved, you have no legal right to ask God for anything except salvation, *(John 9:31)*, even though He may choose to answer you. Why, because you have not accepted Him as your Father. You must first be adopted into His family to claim Him as your own Father, *"For you did not receive the spirit of bondage again to fear, but you received the Spirit of adoption by whom we cry out, "Abba, Father," (Romans 8:15).*

Let us look at it this way, if you work for Company B, why would you expect benefits from Company A for whom you do not work? Company A is not bound by any law to accommodate your needs because you are not on the payroll. So, it is ridiculous to even ask Company A to entertain your unusual request for benefits. Now, why would you ask God for His benefits if you do not love Him enough to give your life to Him and serve Him? Why would He be obligated to bless you or better yet, why would you ask Him for His blessings when you do not trust Him enough to save you from yourself? You must believe on the Lord Jesus Christ to be saved, and if not, there is another alternative, damnation, *"He that believeth and is baptized shall be saved; but he that believeth not shall be damned," (Mark 16:16 KJV).*

Coming to Christ is as simple as A - B - C; *admit* that you are a sinner, *believe* in your heart that God has raised Jesus from the dead and *confess* with your mouth the Lord Jesus and you will be saved, *"that if you confess with your mouth the Lord Jesus and believe in your heart that God has raised Him from the dead, you will be saved. For with the heart one believes unto righteousness, and with the mouth confession is made unto salvation," (Romans 10:9-10).* There are not any other prerequisites to follow or any other rituals to adhere to in order to receive Christ as your Savior.

You can live a victorious life in Christ by simply committing to a relationship with God the Father. He loves you so much that nothing can separate you from His love, *" For I am persuaded that neither death nor life, nor angels nor principalities nor powers, nor things present nor things to come, nor height nor depth, nor any other created thing, shall be able to separate us from the love of God which is in Christ Jesus our Lord," (Romans 8:38-39).*

You could have murdered, peddled drugs, lusted, robbed, cheated, molested, stolen, lied or done any of the other negatives we read about in the newspaper or see on the television day after day; He still loves you and wants you to become a part of His family, no matter what your occupation or status. Jesus knows that you are tired and He wants you to

56

come to Him for rest, *"Come unto me, all ye that labour and are heavy laden, and I will give you rest,"*
(Matthew 11:28 KJV).

So, you see, His love is awesome and there is none that can compare. He is calling to you right now as you are reading this book, *"Seek the LORD while He may be found, Call upon Him while He is near," (Isaiah 55:6)*. Do not go another day without accepting Jesus Christ in your life as your Savior. The rest of this day is not promised to you; choose life now through Jesus Christ before it is too late, *"...Behold now is the accepted time; behold, now is the day of salvation," (2 Corinthians 6:2)*.

If you are now ready to accept the Lord Jesus into your heart and do not know how, please pray this prayer. "Lord God, I admit that I am a sinner, and I want to turn away from sin. I believe in my heart that Jesus died on the cross for my sins, and I also believe that He rose again from the dead and now sits with you in heaven. Jesus, I want You to be the Lord and Savior of my life. I denounce any other god or religion that does not exalt Jesus Christ as Lord of all; I ask that You would fill me with the power of the Holy Spirit. I am now saved from the penalty of sin in Jesus' name, Amen."

Congratulations, this is the most important decision you will ever make in your life......welcome to the family!

Chapter 10

The Holy Spirit

Focus Scripture:

"...And finding some disciples he said to them, "Did you receive the Holy Spirit when you believed." (Acts 19:1-2)

You may believe once you have become a Christian that it is not necessary to be filled with the Holy Spirit. Would you refuse a gift from a loved one simply because you felt you did not need it? Of course you would not! You would accept it and find a way to utilize it. Make no mistake, salvation is unequivocally the greatest gift ever given; receiving the Holy Spirit is like having the ultimate side dish.

Jesus promised that we would do greater works than He, once we were filled with the Holy Spirit, *(John 14:12).* Those who attended Pentecost experienced the filling of the Holy Spirit and were empowered to do the work of Christ. If they were not filled, they would have been powerless against demonic forces. This still applies to us today; if we are not empowered with the Holy Spirit, we will likewise be powerless and not able to boldly go where other anointed people have gone before. This is our opportunity to forge ahead through the endued power from on high, *(Luke 24:49).*

What we must understand is that the gift of the Holy Spirit is not earned for good works, it is simply a gift and gifts are to be received. If we want the filling of the Holy Spirit, we would need to receive Him as our guide. The prerequisite to the filling of the Holy Spirit is first accepting Jesus Christ as Lord and Savior, *(Refer to Chapter 9 on Salvation before continuing with this Chapter)*. Once Christ has been accepted, we are compelled to be filled with the Holy Spirit, *"And do not be drunk with wine, in which is dissipation; but be filled with the Spirit,"* (Ephesians 5:18). Let us look at some of the purposes of the Holy Spirit and why it is so important for us to have Him:

1. **To Assist Us In Witnessing With Words Of Wisdom Without Script**

   But when they arrest you and deliver you up, do not worry beforehand, or premeditate what you will speak. But whatever is given you in that hour, speak that; for it is not you who speak, but the Holy Spirit. (Mark 13:11)

This Scripture was given as an encouragement to the original twelve disciples and others, who faced persecution for the cause of Christ. He promised that the Holy Spirit would serve as a spokesperson for them. Paul was a good example of this Scripture as he completely relied on the Holy Spirit to speak for him as he stood before Agrippa. In

Acts 26:1-29, he recounted his conversion on the road to Damascus.

2. **To Make Us Bold Witnesses For The Love And Power Of Jesus Christ**

But you shall receive power when the Holy Spirit has come upon you; and you shall be witnesses to Me in Jerusalem, and in all Judea and Samaria, and to the end of the earth. (Acts 1:8)

When we are filled with the Holy Spirit, there is a boldness that comes upon us that allows us to share the Gospel of Christ without fear or shame to any and everyone who needs to hear the "Good News." From my experience, this evidence is usually found in those of us who minister street evangelism. Once the boldness through the Holy Spirit is received, it will ultimately change a shy convert into a bold witness for the kingdom of God.

3. **To Intercede For Us And Through Us According To God's Will**

Likewise the Spirit also helps in our weaknesses. For we do not know what we should pray for as we ought, but the Spirit Himself makes intercession for us with groanings which cannot be uttered. Now He who searches the hearts knows what the mind of the Spirit is, because He makes intercession for the saints according to the will of God (Romans 8:26-27).

Just face it. We really do not know how to pray or for what to pray. Thank God for assistance in getting our prayers answered. Perhaps, we may pray for selfish things and possibly things that are not in the will of God, *(James 4:3),* but the Holy Spirit is there to help us in our weaknesses through groanings of no clarity; nonetheless, the prayer is carried to the Father on our behalf.

4. **To Make Us Christ-Like**
He who says he abides in Him ought himself also to walk just as He walked. (1 John 2:6)

We should do all that we can to live like Christ as we walk in His footsteps. He provided the perfect example for us to duplicate. Although it is difficult sometimes to keep up the pace, "*. . . My strength is made perfect in weakness...,*"
(2 Corinthians 12:9), through Jesus Christ. We can make it if we continue to press.

5. **To Seal Those Who Have Been Regenerated**
In Him you also trusted, after you heard the word of truth, the gospel of your salvation; in whom also, having believed, you were sealed with the Holy Spirit of promise, who is the guarantee of our inheritance until the redemption of the purchased possession, to the praise of His glory (Ephesians 1:13-14).

We have been purchased by God and assured an inheritance. From salvation to the day of redemption, the Holy Spirit, as a prized possession of God has sealed us. We are no longer separated from God, but brought into union with Him through the sealing of His promise.

6. **To Bear Witness Of Jesus Christ As He Convicts Hearts Of The Truth**
But when the Helper comes, whom I shall send to you from the Father, the Spirit of truth who proceeds from the Father, He will testify of Me. And you also will bear witness, because you have been with Me from the beginning (John 15:26-27).

The Holy Spirit serves as what I like to call a Public Relations Specialist for Jesus Christ. He will open the heart of a sinner to the truth about the existence of the risen Savior. The Holy Spirit will also communicate with a sinner in a way that He convicts his heart concerning the truth of his sinful nature. He will also tug and pull on his mind to beg him to repent of his sins. The Holy Spirit will furthermore make the sinner aware that He will convict the world of sin, righteousness, and of judgment, because people refuse to believe in Jesus, *(John 16:8)*.

Now that you are aware of some of the responsibilities of the Holy Spirit, you can now receive Him. The prerequisite to receiving the Holy Spirit has already been given and that is first receiving Christ in your heart. Then you must surrender full control of your will, mind, tongue, body and every part of your being to the Holy Spirit. He must have your permission in order to live within you as your Comforter and your Guide. He will not share you with another spirit; He wants to have full possession. Once He has complete dominion over you, He will speak through you in a heavenly language, which is the evidence that He reigns and rules in your life.

For this reason, many denominations feel that those who are in the Baptist faith are going to hell for all eternity because many Baptist deny the need to receive the Holy Spirit. Although many do not receive the Holy Spirit, there are those not only in the Baptist faith but also other various denominations who graciously receive the Holy Spirit. Therefore anyone who passes judgment on another believers' acceptance will ultimately answer to God. Receive Him today.

If you are now ready to receive the Holy Spirit, pray this prayer. "Holy Spirit, I want You to take over my life, mind, body, will, nature, tongue, and every part of my being. I relinquish full control to You as You fill me. I surrender completely to Your authority and trust that You will guide me throughout eternity with those things that are good, true and perfect. I welcome the Holy Spirit of God, I welcome Your dominion. I now receive You as my teacher, my ruler, and my guide, in Jesus' name, Amen."

Chapter 11

Healing

Focus Scripture:

"But He was wounded for our transgressions, He was bruised for our iniquities; The chastisement for our peace was upon Him, And by His stripes we are healed."
(Isaiah 53:5)

Many have sought various antidotes and formulas to receive healing for what ails them. Based on the above Scripture, Jesus bore all of our infirmities, sicknesses and diseases on the cross. All we have to do is believe and receive that His stripes have guaranteed our healing and it shall be done. This means we do not have to take our own burden of illnesses, because Jesus took our place so that we could live a life of wholeness.

Please be aware that even during Jesus' ministry, there were some people who were not healed. There are those who will never receive healing for their sickness because they do not believe that they can be healed. One instance of this fact was when Jesus had difficulty healing in His own hometown because of the unbelief of the people, *(Mark 6:1-6)*. They did not see Him as Jesus, the Healer they only saw Him as Jesus,

Mary's son. If they had believed, more people would have been healed.

Consequently, do not lose heart or feel that God is not going to heal your condition. Focus on the many times that He did heal; such as, the man who was born blind, and Jesus made clay out of spittle and dirt to heal his blindness, (*John 9:1-7*); and the woman who had an issue of blood for twelve years, when she touched Jesus' garment and was instantly healed, (*Mark 5:25-34*); also a man in the synagogue with a withered hand, who was healed on the Sabbath, (*Matthew 12:9-13*); and also the ten lepers, who were cleansed as they went to show themselves to the priest, (*Luke 17:11-19*); then the nobleman's son healed by Jesus simply speaking the Word, (*John 4:46-50*); and then the woman bowed over for eighteen years, and Jesus spoke the Word, laid His hands on her and she was immediately healed, (*Luke 13:10-13*). These sicknesses and diseases all ended in success as well as so many other healing miracles listed in the New Testament, which were performed by Jesus, His disciples, and other prophets.

Another occasion of healing was in *Mark 2:1-12*, when four persistent people carried a paralytic to Jesus to be healed of his infirmity. Jesus verified His authenticity as the Son of man by forgiving the paralyzed man of his sins and told him to take up his bed and walk. Of course, it is just like

Jesus to treat the entire person's ills. He not only healed his body, but He also healed his soul. Jesus did not offer just a temporary fix of physical healing because it may have resulted in a reoccurrence of the same sickness but he fixed the entire man.

If you believe that your sickness is a result of unconfessed sin, be big enough to confess it right now to God and then anyone else who may be involved, *(Refer to Chapter 3 on Unforgiveness),* and the Lord will raise you up. You must also speak words of victory not defeat. Do not let others speak words of damnation or death to you about the condition you have. You have the power to speak life or death to your surroundings, *(Proverbs 18:21)*, so just speak life. The Word of God will bring life to your dead circumstance, *(1 John 1:1)*.

I can recall waking up early one morning with symptoms of a virus. My stomach was twisted and all of the other symptoms that accompany a virus were also present; I felt miserable. I remembered that I had to teach a Bible study class that evening and soon realized that I would not be able to find anyone to substitute for me at the last minute. I then began to speak words of life such as *"Lord, You've healed all of my diseases," (Psalm 103:3)*, and *"by Your stripes I'm healed," (Isaiah 53:5)*, then I drifted off to sleep.

When I woke later that evening, I had enough strength to get to class, but I was still moving slowly. Once class started, I began to speak on the topic, "Faith," and how it moves God and strengthens the walk of the believer. All of a sudden, something began to happen to me as I spoke. I felt this unexplained strength inside as though the symptoms were drying up. Needless to say, when class was dismissed, so was the virus that I had had all day. I was healed through teaching the Word of God because it brought life to my body. I received the finished work of Jesus Christ that was done on Calvary!!

Even though you may not see the immediate results, continue to thank God for what His Word has promised and believe what you decree, for He will establish it, *"You will also declare a thing, And it will be established for you; So light will shine on your ways," (Job 22:28).* Your words are so important to your existence.

Now this story is an interesting one. Early on in ministry, I discovered that God can heal your enemy even if you do not want them to be healed. Yes, I said it. There was a woman who was ridiculously unkind to me. She started rumors about me which were untrue and shared with me some of the ugly things that she told other people about me. Of course, this caused me to be a little bitter with her. One day she asked me to pray for her because she had an infirmity that governed her life for some time. Because of how she abused my name, I did not want to pray for her healing. So, I touched her for a few seconds and said, *"Be Healed in Jesus Name,"* and I was done. In my small thinking, I thought that God was going to ignore my prayer because I did not want her to be healed. However, I received a surprise. Sometime later, she told me that she was completely healed of her infirmity and she wanted to thank God for using me to pray for her healing. Now, I was mad at God because He healed her as wicked as she had been to me. I felt that He should have denied her healing because of how she treated me. Consequently, I cried out to God and asked Him why did He heal her? To my surprise, He told me that I do not preach about myself but of Jesus Christ because the excellency of the power is of Him and not of me (2 Corinthians 4)." He basically told me that I was the earthen vessel being used for a Divine purpose …it was not about me or what I wanted but about the work of the kingdom. It was then that I dried up my tears and said no more about that situation. Healing comes from God not from mankind. He chooses to heal, however it is up to the individual to receive the finished work on Calvary even though someone may stand in opposition.

Although the devil will try to bring sickness and disease your way, you have the Word of God as your weapon of defense against these illnesses. If you still do not have enough faith to believe God for healing, begin building your faith through this method: whenever you feel a headache or a stomach cramp trying to take over your body, put your hand on the spot and speak to the pain in the name of Jesus and believe by faith that it is already done, because it is. The healing may be instant or it may be gradual, but whatever way it leaves, be thankful that it is done. Although this sounds like a small feat, it will increase your faith each time you are victorious, then you can progress to larger challenges as they appear. Even if you find that some healings are instantaneous and others may be over a period of time, please continue to practice standing on the promises of God for your healing.

Jesus healed in biblical times and He will still heal today. He is one that changes not, *"Jesus Christ is the same yesterday, today, and forever," (Hebrews 13:8)*. My friend, believe that God wants you to be whole, *(3 John 2)*. It is up to you to receive what He has already done for you on Calvary over 2000 years ago.

Pray this prayer to be healed of your infirmity. "Lord God, You are Jehovah-Ropheka, the Lord that heals me, and I believe by faith that You bore all of my infirmities on the cross. I receive my healing from all of my infirmities and/or diseases, which are hindering my progress, and I thank You for my healing. In Jesus' name, Amen."

Chapter 12

Freedom

Focus Scripture:

"Therefore if the Son makes you free, you shall be free indeed." (John 8:36)

It is 5:30 a.m., the alarm clock just rang, and you are lying in the bed feeling spiritually incapacitated. You whimper silently because of your inability to communicate exactly how you feel internally. You think to yourself, "here we go again, same ole' same ole', just a different day." You then go about your way getting prepared for work, and then you look into the mirror only to think of more ways to continue to hide the inner turmoil that has been festering for decades.

It is no secret that we have all been through tough times, but I have found, through the experience of counseling those who suffer from sexual or mental abuse at a young age, they have many layers of hurt to overcome and their past seems to haunt their present. Yes, they look good from a distance but they have become a recluse as they quietly withdraw from society, family and friends because of past hurt. Sometimes they even hide behind walls of anger and bitterness as they lash out at others. When approached, inferiority rises within them as they inwardly cry out for restitution.

This was true in the case of a young lady with whom I had the opportunity to lead to deliverance. When she was a youth, a family member molested her. She knew it was wrong, but she did not quite know how to prevent it from happening again or how she could stop it from disturbing her thoughts. So, like thousands of others, she suppressed her thoughts, which was the worst thing she could have done. She did not feel that anyone would care, nor would anything happen to the offender even if she told her story.

She was very outgoing and loved to mingle with people, but she was hiding a lot of hurt and unforgiveness back in the corridors of her heart. As time went on, she strived to look for love from a variety of men, but soon found that they, much like the offender of her past, did not really love her at all. After a series of so-called "love affairs", she found that her appetite for affection grew so strong that each sexual encounter was not enough to feed the erotic behavior to which she was accustomed. She could not reach the pinnacle of her sexual desires through "normal" means. As she continued to search for contentment, her sexual preference soon changed from men to women. She was getting buried deeper and deeper in a sinful rut of no return.

72

Other areas of her life were in severe ruins and she did not know how to stop this vicious cycle. She hurtfully stated that she is only trying to find love, but so often she seemed to confuse love with lust as she willingly prostituted herself.

She could never make any real friends nor have lasting relationships due to her promiscuity. Respectful women would not be caught around her because of her checkered past. They treated her as a cancer and would not be caught talking to her for fear of association. Oh, by the way, did I mention that this young lady was a Christian and worked faithfully in a church? Yes, she was in bondage and wanted to be free.

In hearing this cry out for freedom from this young lady, I was reminded of a similar story in the New Testament about the woman at the well, *(John 4:7-18)*. She had been married five times, and then she was also living with a man which was not her husband. The women of the town no doubt condemned her because of her promiscuous lifestyle, but she was obviously sought after by men who did not mind using her for their pleasures. Even though others may have segregated themselves from her, Jesus still had a need to go through Samaria just to minister to her needs. The Bible never suggested that she was abused at an early age however her past gave a dim light for her future prosperities, much like this young lady.

I shared with the young lady that Jesus wanted to heal her internal wounds. I explained to her that from my observation, I have found that those who have been sexually abused or exposed to sexual abuse suffer spiritual and emotional trauma. This unfortunately opens doorways in the victim's life which causes rejection, abandonment and other demonic forces to take residence. That is when the masquerade begins in order to hide the internal pain. Many times the victim chooses an iniquitous path, which may include pedophilia, homosexuality, multiple sex partners, bestiality or other unnatural pleasures, which are abominations to God. This is a deception of the devil.

This was her moment to turn her entire life around for the better. She wanted to be released from the invisible prison in which she had been living in for so many years. We began to pray that she would first be able to forgive the one who abused her, the one who was supposed to protect her and also to forgive herself. She tearfully asked God to mend the broken pieces of her life that had been scattered abroad. After many hours of confession and prayer, she was delivered from the cesspool of her past and was ready for the next assignment that God had for her.

Since there are those who would still point the finger and gossip about her past, this Scripture comes to mind, *"Who shall bring a charge against God's elect? It is God who justifies. Who is he who condemns? It is Christ who died, and furthermore is also risen, who is even at the right hand of God, who also makes intercession for us,"* (Romans 8:33-34). Ain't that good news?

Just think; no one can hold any charge against you because of the grace and justification of God, just as if you have never sinned. Let that sink in; no one can ever condemn you of your raunchy past because Jesus' precious blood covers all of your wrong doings once you have accepted Him as Lord of your life. If you stand in need of deliverance of this nature, there is a successful ending for you too. Although you may be privately hurting from your past, God knows all of your hurts, and He wants to heal them. Why not let Him help you with your current?

Pray this prayer to receive freedom. "Lord God, I have been in bondage for so long and I need to be free from my prison of isolation. Please help me to forgive others and to forgive myself. Heal my internal wounds and allow me to breathe again without feeling pressure. Please remove the stench of my past from the corridors of my memory as I receive my freedom that You promised through Jesus Christ, in Jesus' name, Amen."

Chapter 13

Prosperity God's Way

Focus Scripture:

"Give, and it will be given to you: good measure, pressed down, shaken together, and running over will be put into your bosom. For with the same measure that you use, it will be measured back to you." (Luke 6:38)

The secret of gaining wealth is more than just attending seminars and conferences to find out how to become wealthy. There are so many books and lessons you can buy which may give you pointers on how to attain great riches, but few to any on how to bless others once you have attained great riches.

There are some people who will play bingo or the lottery and they will also visit all of the gambling hot spots in hopes of striking it rich. I have even had a woman to tell me that she really does not gamble to be wealthy, but she just likes the "excitement of winning." Yeah, ok; I thought. What a sorry excuse to cover up an addiction, which is also another area that could stand deliverance. Is this you?

As I laughingly look back over several years, I can remember a time when I was addicted to pyramid groups and network marketing, which were considered "get rich quick" schemes. Every commercial that came on television concerning making money, caught my attention. My eyes would get big as quarters when I listened to the testimonials of others who had made a small fortune selling a product. I found myself ordering kits of merchandise and products that I had never used or heard of before, but I was going to sell it to others to make my own fortune.

I spent a busload of money that I did not have, on somebody else's idea just to make a quick buck. I peddled diet products, household chemicals, 800 numbers, jewelry and so many other items, trying to get rich quickly. But unfortunately, I lost more money getting involved than I actually received. The infomercials never advised me that customers would stiff me on payments, give me bad checks, or better yet say that they will pay me when they get their next pay check, which sometimes was never; then I was stuck with boxes of products because the return policy of a so called thirty-day guarantee just ran out the day before I got frustrated. After losing thousands of dollars, and taking several Tylenol #3 tablets, I then realized, if I prospered God's way, it would come without sorrow, (*Proverbs 10:22*).

In that, I tried to make my own wealth because of my selfish desires; and I received all of the anxiety that came along with it. I had to face reality and confirm that this was not the way in which God wanted me to enter into financial wealth. I was not committed to the agenda of God, but I wanted riches to buy a new house, new pairs of shoes, perhaps a new car, but nothing for anyone else, including the work of God. I have finally learned to prosper God's way!

The quicker we realize that it is the will of God that a Christian prospers financially, physically and spiritually, the better off we will be, *(3 John 2)*. God, our Father, has sanctioned these blessings, why not become a recipient of the promise? I am aware that some of us have been taught that if we were true Christians, we should be poor, as Jesus was poor. But the true fact is, Jesus was a carpenter by trade and was not by any means impoverished. During His ministry, He chose to leave His home in Nazareth, leave all behind and trust God for His daily needs. Jesus did not allow anything to hinder His ministry. Even today many speak ill of preachers who live in nice homes and drive nice cars because it is felt that ministers should take a vow of poverty. Often it is said that they are stealing money from those who are poor. Although this may or may not be true, Jesus was able to avoid this type of ridicule.

There is no law against having money, but there is a law against loving the money in which we have. For the Bible says, *"For the love of money is a root of all kinds of evil, for which some have strayed from the faith in their greediness, and pierced themselves through with many sorrows,"*

(1 Timothy 6:10). So you see, it is not having money that is evil, but the love of it. The love of money will have our faith based on the provision instead of the Provider.

There is a better way to gain wealth without wasting all of our money on various lotto games and pyramid ventures. Yes, it is quite simple. Let us briefly look at some principles that will help us prosper the way that God intended:

1. **Be Obedient To God's Word**

There is great responsibility that comes along with the blessings of God, *"For everyone to whom much is given, from him much will be required; and to whom much has been committed, of him they will ask the more,"* *(Luke 12:48).* When God has revealed His will through His Word to us, we are obligated to obey what has been exposed. God will hold us accountable for the knowledge of His Word. Listed below are a few requirements of being obedient to God's Word:

> a. **Accept Jesus Christ as Lord and Savior, (Romans 10:9-10)**

Of course, these are not the only requirements in the Word in which to be obedient, but they will give us a head start. We welcome poverty to reign in our lives when we are disobedient. When we deny Christ to be the Lord of our life, we forego all of the benefits that we could inherit as a child of the King. The free gift of salvation is so easy to receive and He offers it to all *(Refer to Chapter 9 on Salvation)*. Accepting Jesus in our hearts will not only open the door to eternal life, but it will also open the avenues for prosperity right here on earth.

b. **Love God And Also One Another, (Matthew 22:37-40)**

The two great commandments instruct us not only to love the Lord with all that is within us but also to love our neighbor as ourselves. I have found through life's experiences that most of us love ourselves, sometimes to an abnormal degree. This may cause us to become self-centered if much care is not taken. The Lord is simply asking for us to love Him with our entire being, which means more than we love ourselves, and likewise to love others.

c. **Do Not Rob God Of What Belongs To Him, (Malachi 3:7-12)**

Although under the Old Testament law, *Malachi 3:7-12* relates how Israel turned from the ordinances of God. They had robbed Him of His tithes and offerings. God further told them that they were cursed with a curse because of this act. This Scripture is not centered on their giving as much as it is centered on their obedience to the law of God. God did not give these guidelines just because He had nothing better to do. He gave guidelines to bless His children through obedience to Him.

If we are obedient to His Word, He has even promised to rebuke the devourer for our sake, so that the fruit of our ground may prosper. When we rob God of what is due Him, we will rob ourselves of the blessings that He wants to present to us. God will always reward us when we are obedient. That is His Word!

d. **Stay Legal By Paying Your Taxes, (Mark 12:13-17)**

Since biblical days, it seems that the word "taxes" have been perceived as a dirty word. This area is a touchy subject matter in most of our homes and churches. Some of us feel that taxes are not biblical nor should Christians be mandated to pay them. Whether we are Christians or not, we are held accountable when we are disobedient to the laws of the land, and we will not escape God's punishment if we are caught lacking.

In the above Scripture, the Herodians and a segment of Pharisees were sent to trick Jesus into saying that there was no need to pay taxes (give tribute) to Caesar. Perhaps they did not want to pay taxes at all and wanted Jesus to be the scapegoat of approval. But because Jesus knew their wicked thoughts, He asked for a coin to allow them to see whose inscription was printed thereon, and delivered His answer accordingly. To their surprise, He did not tell them not to pay taxes, but He advised them to pay what is required to whom payment is due.

Over the years, things have not changed. Some people still do not believe in paying taxes to the IRS, because they lie about their income on their tax returns. This is direct disobedience to the law of the land and to the Word of God.

2. **Giving From Your Substance**

Money is made to be recycled. One infallible way of prospering God's way would be through our giving. *"Give, and it will be given to you: good measure, pressed down, shaken together, and running over will be put into your bosom. For with the same measure that you use, it will be measured back to you," (Luke 6:38).* It may sound backwards to first give from our resources then wait to receive the reward, but it is the order of God. He wants nothing less for us than to bless us with a degree of abundance.

I remember some time ago, expressing to a minister how I wanted to be a blessing to other people financially, but it seemed as though I did not quite have enough to spare. The minister responded to me with a basic principle, which is sometimes considered insane to some. He told me to give from my substance and watch the Lord replenish what I had given. He began to explain how he had utilized this principle for years and was astonished by the way in which God had blessed him. He stated that money was coming to him from places he had never expected a return. So I decided to give from my substance, even though it seemed like I did not have much to offer; and to my amazement the Lord not only prospered me financially, but also in many other areas of my life. It really worked!

I have received many testimonies from people who shared how God multiplied their money after they had sown financial seeds into the lives of others. They felt that it was better than investing in the market.

With this in mind, we should realize that the way we calculate return is not the way God calculates return, Amen! We never know how He is going to bless us. When we plant a faith seed, there is more than just a leaf that will grow; for we will reap a harvest, or better yet, trees with several branches. Who could fathom such a thought? It is difficult to grasp the way in which God thinks, *"For My thoughts are not your thoughts, Nor are your ways My ways," says the Lord. "For as the heavens are higher than the earth, So are My ways higher than your ways, And My thoughts than your thoughts," (Isaiah 55:8-9).*

I am a believer that when we take care of the work that God has called us to do, He will take care of our needs *(Philippians 4:19).* The widow was blessed beyond measure when she made a cake for the prophet Elijah. Her intentions were to use the last of her meal and oil for herself and her son then they was going to die because there would be none left. However, because she gave first, to the prophet, the Bible says that her household ate for many days thereafter, *(1 Kings 17:8-16)*.

There is a blessing in giving. We will stifle our blessings by holding on to what we think belongs to us instead of sharing with others. What we have does not belong to us anyway, it belongs to the Lord, *"The earth is the LORD'S, and all its fullness, the world and those who dwell therein," (Psalm 24:1)*. He has only made us stewards over the possessions that He has given us. When we have our fist closed tightly, nothing can get out of it to neither bless others, nor can anything get in it to bless us. Let us keep our hands open for God to make a deposit.

If you are searching for prosperity and wealth, you will not find it in the state's lotto. Stop wasting your money on conferences and seminars that do not teach prosperity by the principles of God. Just simply began to be obedient to God's Word and condition your mind to give in order to help others, especially to world missions, where you can assist others in distributing the Gospel to the nations. When you follow God's guidelines, whatsoever you do shall prosper, *(Psalm 1:3)*. Do not give till it hurts; give till it feels good!

Pray this prayer to receive prosperity God's way. "Lord God, I am now aware that poverty is a curse and has robbed me of my financial blessings. Help me learn to give unselfishly to others and show me where to sow seeds to enhance the kingdom. You promised in *Matthew 6:33*, that if I would seek Your kingdom first, then You would add everything else that I need. I receive prosperity as one of my benefits as a born again believer, I am no longer under the curse of the law anymore in Jesus' name, Amen."

Chapter 14

God's Promises & Declarations

Focus Scripture:

"For all the promises of God in Him are Yes, and in Him Amen, to the glory of God through us." (2 Corinthians 1:20)

A promise is known as a statement binding the one who makes the guarantee. God's promises are Yes and Amen, *(2 Corinthians 1:20),* through satisfaction in Jesus Christ. He promises that *"Heaven and earth will pass away, but My words will by no means pass away," (Mark 13:31).* Just knowing when God promises us something through His Word, it will come to pass before heaven and earth passes away, that is good news!

Through experiences in life, we find that every Scripture is God-breathed and has been written to fit every facet of our lives, in order to equip and complete us, *"All Scripture is given by inspiration of God, and is profitable for doctrine, for reproof, for correction, for instruction in righteousness, that the man of God may be complete, thoroughly equipped for every good work,"*
(2 Timothy 3:16-17). Whatever assurance God has given in His Word, He is obligated to bless us with what He has

promised. As we continue to believe by faith, we are entitled to receive His blessings.

It may seem mysterious as to why God loves us so much to make promises over two thousand years ago that would apply to us today. It may even seem as though God's promises will never come to pass for us, but that is when our faith should step in and realize, *"But as it is written: Eye has not seen, nor ear heard, Nor have entered into the heart of man The things which God has prepared for those who love Him," (1 Corinthians 2:9).*

There are those of whom I have heard say, "God said it, I believe it, and that settles it." What a strong declaration of faith? However, there are times that one may wonder, is that really what is believed deep within their spirit, or is it just another popular phrase or catchy cliché to twist the ears of the surrounding crowd? Many times their faith turns out to be contradictory because of their actions.

Let us start today believing by faith that we are entitled to receive the promises of God, and then watch them manifest. Here are some of the promises and declarations God has made to us for all of our needs...

Authority

"When the righteous are in authority, the people rejoice; But when a wicked man rules, the people groan."
(Proverbs 29:2)

"Then He called His twelve disciples together and gave them power and authority over all demons, and to cure diseases."
(Luke 9:1)

"Behold, I give you the authority to trample on serpents and scorpions, and over all the power of the enemy, and nothing shall by any means hurt you."
(Luke 10:19)

"Having disarmed principalities and powers, He made a public spectacle of them, triumphing over them in it."
(Colossians 2:15)

"There is also an antitype which now saves us-baptism (not the removal of the filth of the flesh, but the answer of a good conscience toward God), through the resurrection of Jesus Christ, who has gone into heaven and is at the right hand of God, angels and authorities and powers having been made subject to Him."
(1 Peter 3:21-22)

Children

"Out of the mouth of babes and nursing infants You have ordained strength, Because of Your enemies, That You may silence the enemy and the avenger." (Psalm 8:2)
"Behold, children are a heritage from the LORD, The fruit of the womb is a reward."
(Psalm 127:3)

"Train up a child in the way he should go, And when he is old he will not depart from it."
(Proverbs 22:6)

"For the promise is to you and to your children, and to all who are afar off, as many as the Lord our God will call."
(Acts 2:39)

"Children, obey your parents in the Lord, for this is right. 'Honor your father and mother,' which is the first commandment with promise: "that it may be well with you and you may live long on the earth."
(Ephesians 6:1-3)

Favor

"But the LORD was with Joseph and showed him mercy, and He gave him favor in the sight of the keeper of the prison."
(Genesis 39:21)

"For You, O LORD, will bless the righteous; With favor You will surround him as with a shield."
(Psalm 5:12)

"He who earnestly seeks good finds favor, But trouble will come to him who seeks evil."
(Proverbs 11:27)

"A good man obtains favor from the LORD, But a man of wicked intentions He will condemn."
(Proverbs 12:2)

Fear

"And Moses said to the people, "Do not be afraid. Stand still, and see the salvation of the LORD, which He will accomplish for you today. For the Egyptians whom you see today, you shall see again no more forever."
(Exodus 14:13)

"Then Joshua said to them, "Do not be afraid, nor be dismayed; be strong and of good courage, for thus the LORD will do to all your enemies against whom you fight."
(Joshua 10:25)

"When you lie down, you will not be afraid; Yes, you will lie down and your sleep will be sweet."
(Proverbs 3:24)

"For I, the LORD your God, will hold your right hand, Saying to you, 'Fear not, I will help you.'"
(Isaiah 41:13)

"For God has not given us a spirit of fear, but of power and of love and of a sound mind."
(2 Timothy 1:7)

"So we may boldly say: "The LORD is my helper; I will not fear. What can man do to me?"
 (Hebrews 13:6)

"There is no fear in love; but perfect love casts out fear, because fear involves torment. But he who fears has not been made perfect in love."
(1 John 4:18)

Forgiveness

"Do not say, "I will recompense evil"; Wait for the LORD, and He will save you."
(Proverbs 20:22)

"For if you forgive men their trespasses, your heavenly Father will also forgive you."
(Matthew 6:14)

"And whenever you stand praying, if you have anything against anyone, forgive him that your Father in heaven may also forgive you, your trespasses."
(Mark 11:25)

"Take heed to yourselves. If your brother sins against you, rebuke him; and if he repents, forgive him. And if he sins against you seven times in a day, and seven times in a day returns to you, saying, 'I repent', you shall forgive him."
(Luke 17:3-4)

"Therefore "If your enemy is hungry, feed him; If he is thirsty, give him a drink; For in so doing you will heap coals of fire on his head."
(Romans 12:20)

Grieving

"Yea, though I walk through the valley of the shadow of death, I will fear no evil; For You are with me; Your rod and Your staff, they comfort me."
(Psalm 23:4)

"The LORD is good, A stronghold in the day of trouble; And He knows those who trust in Him."
(Nahum 1:7)

"Blessed are those who mourn, For they shall be comforted."
(Matthew 5:4)

"For we do not have a High Priest who cannot sympathize with our weaknesses, but was in all points tempted as we are, yet without sin. Let us therefore come boldly to the throne of grace that we may obtain mercy and find grace to help in time of need."
(Hebrews 4:15-16)

"And God will wipe away every tear from their eyes; there shall be no more death, nor sorrow, nor crying. There shall be no more pain, for the former things have passed away."
(Revelation 21:4)

Guidance

"I will instruct you and teach you in the way you should go; I will guide you with My eye."
(Psalm 32:8)

"A man's heart plans his way, But the LORD directs his steps."
(Proverbs 16:9)

"Your ears shall hear a word behind you, saying, "This is the way, walk in it," Whenever you turn to the right hand Or whenever you turn to the left."
(Isaiah 30:21)

"The LORD will guide you continually, And satisfy your soul in drought, And strengthen your bones; You shall be like a watered garden, And like a spring of water, whose waters do not fail."
(Isaiah 58:11)

"However, when He, the Spirit of truth, has come, He will guide you into all truth; for He will not speak on His own authority, but whatever He hears He will speak; and He will tell you things to come."
(John 16:13)

Healing

"Bless the LORD, O my soul, And forget not all His benefits: Who forgives all your iniquities, Who heals all your diseases."
(Psalm 103:2-3)

"The spirit of a man will sustain him in sickness, But who can bear a broken spirit?"
(Proverbs 18:14)

"But He was wounded for our transgressions, He was bruised for our iniquities; The chastisement for our peace was upon Him, And by His stripes we are healed."
(Isaiah 53:5)

"And these signs will follow those who believe: In My name they will cast out demons; they will speak with new tongues; they will take up serpents; and if they drink anything deadly, it will by no means hurt them; they will lay hands on the sick, and they will recover."
(Mark 16:17-18)

"Also a multitude gathered from the surrounding cities to Jerusalem, bringing sick people and those who were tormented by unclean spirits, and they were all healed."
(Acts 5:16)

"And the prayer of faith will save the sick, and the Lord will raise him up. And if he has committed sins, he will be forgiven. Confess your trespasses to one another, and pray for one another, that you may be healed. The effective, fervent prayer of a righteous man avails much."
(James 5:15-16)

Humility

"Surely He scorns the scornful, But gives grace to the humble."
(Proverbs 3:34)

"Therefore whoever humbles himself as this little child is the greatest in the kingdom of heaven."
(Matthew 18:4)

"But "he who glories, let him glory in the LORD." For not he who commends himself is approved, but who the Lord commends."
(2 Corinthians 10:17-18)

"I, therefore, the prisoner of the Lord, beseech you to walk worthy of the calling with which you were called, with all lowliness and gentleness, with longsuffering, bearing with one another in love, endeavoring to keep the unity of the Spirit in the bond of peace."
(Ephesians 4:1-3)

"Likewise you younger people, submit yourselves to your elders. Yes, all of you be submissive to one another, and be clothed with humility, for "God resists the proud, But gives grace to the humble." Therefore humble yourselves under the mighty hand of God, that He may exalt you in due time, casting all your care upon Him, for He cares for you."
(1 Peter 5:5-6)

Joy

"You have put gladness in my heart, More than in the season that their grain and wine increased."
(Psalm 4:7)

"To console those who mourn in Zion, To give them beauty for ashes, The oil of joy for mourning, The garment of praise for the spirit of heaviness; That they may be called trees of righteousness, The planting of the LORD, that He may be glorified."
(Isaiah 61:3)

"Yet I will rejoice in the LORD, I will joy in the God of my salvation."
(Habakkuk 3:18)

"Therefore you now have sorrow; but I will see you again and your heart will rejoice, and your joy no one will take from you."
(John 16:22)

"For what is our hope, or joy, or crown of rejoicing? Is it not even you in the presence of our Lord Jesus Christ at His coming? For you are our glory and joy."
(1 Thessalonians 2:19-20)

Love

"For God so loved the world that He gave His only begotten Son, that whoever believes in Him should not perish but have everlasting life."
(John 3:16)

"Let love be without hypocrisy. Abhor what is evil. Cling to what is good. Be kindly affectionate to one another with brotherly love, in honor giving preference to one another."
(Romans 12:9-10)

"Though I speak with the tongues of men and of angels, but have not love, I have become sounding brass or a clanging cymbal. And though I have the gift of prophecy, and understand all mysteries and all knowledge, and though I have all faith, so that I could remove mountains, but have not love, I am nothing. And though I bestow all my goods to feed the poor, and though I give my body to be burned, but have not love, it profits me nothing."
(1 Corinthians 13:1-3)

"Let brotherly love continue."
 (Hebrews 13:1)

"If you really fulfill the royal law according to the Scripture, "You shall love your neighbor as yourself, you do well; but if you show partiality, you commit sin, and are convicted by the law as transgressors."
(James 2:8-9)

"My little children, let us not love in word or in tongue, but in deed and in truth."
(1 John 3:18)

Obedience

"Therefore keep the words of this covenant, and do them, that you may prosper in all that you do."
(Deuteronomy 29:9)

"Blessed are those who keep justice, And he who does righteousness at all times!"
(Psalm 106:3)

"Not everyone who says to Me, 'Lord, Lord,' shall enter the kingdom of heaven, but he who does the will of My Father in heaven."
(Matthew 7:21)

"Most assuredly, I say to you, if anyone keeps My word he shall never see death."
(John 8:51)

"The things which you learned and received and heard and saw in me, these do, and the God of peace will be with you."
(Philippians 4:9)

"And having been perfected, He became the author of eternal salvation to all who obey Him." (Hebrews 5:9)

Patience

"The LORD is good to those who wait for Him, To the soul who seeks Him. It is good that one should hope and wait quietly For the salvation of the LORD."
(Lamentations 3:25-26)

"But if we hope for what we do not see, we eagerly wait for it with perseverance."
(Romans 8:25)

"And let us not grow weary while doing good, for in due season we shall reap if we do not lose heart."
(Galatians 6:9)

"And we desire that each one of you show the same diligence to the full assurance of hope until the end, that you do not become sluggish, but imitate those who through faith and patience inherit the promises."
(Hebrews 6:11-12)

"Therefore do not cast away your confidence, which has great reward. For you have need of endurance, so that after you have done the will of God, you may receive the promise."
(Hebrews 10:35-36)

"But let patience have its perfect work, that you may be perfect and complete, lacking nothing."
(James 1:4)

Peace

"The LORD will fight for you, and you shall hold your peace."
(Exodus 14:14)

"When a man's ways please the LORD, He makes even his enemies to be at peace with him."
(Proverbs 16:7)

"You will keep him in perfect peace, Whose mind is stayed on You, Because he trusts in You."
(Isaiah 26:3)

"Blessed are the peacemakers, For they shall be called sons of God."
(Matthew 5:9)

"Therefore, having been justified by faith, we have peace with God through our Lord Jesus Christ, through whom also we have access by faith into this grace in which we stand, and rejoice in hope of the glory of God."
(Romans 5:1-2)

"Be anxious for nothing, but in everything by prayer and supplication, with thanksgiving, let your requests be made known to God; and the peace of God, which surpasses all understanding, will guard your hearts and minds through Christ Jesus."
(Philippians 4:6-7)

Position/Status

"You will also declare a thing, And it will be established for you; So light will shine on your ways."
(Job 22:28)

"A man's gift makes room for him, And brings him before great men."
(Proverbs 18:16)

"By humility and the fear of the LORD Are riches and honor and life."
(Proverbs 22:4)

Prayer

"Evening and morning and at noon I will pray, and cry aloud, And He shall hear my voice."
(Psalm 55:17)

"The LORD is near to all who call upon Him, To all who call upon Him in truth."
(Psalm 145:18)

"The LORD is far from the wicked, But He hears the prayer of the righteous."
(Proverbs 15:29)

"Thus says the LORD who made it, the LORD who formed it to establish it (the LORD is His name): 'Call to Me, and I will answer you, and show you great and mighty things, which you do not know.'"
(Jeremiah 33:2-3)

"If you abide in Me, and My words abide in you, you will ask what you desire, and it shall be done for you."
(John 15:7)

Prosperity

"This Book of the Law shall not depart from your mouth, but you shall meditate in it day and night, that you may observe to do according to all that is written in it. For then you will make your way prosperous, and then you will have good success."
(Joshua 1:8)

"The Lord has been mindful of us; He will bless us; He will bless the house of Israel; He will bless the house of Aaron. He will bless those who fear the LORD, Both small and great. May the LORD give you increase more and more, You and your children."
(Psalm 115:12-14)

"Bring all the tithes into the storehouse, That there may be food in My house, And try Me now in this, Says the LORD of hosts, If I will not open for you the windows of heaven And pour out for you such blessing That there will not be room enough to receive it. And I will rebuke the devourer for your sakes, So that he will not destroy the fruit of your ground, Nor shall the vine fail to bear fruit for you in the field, "Says the LORD of hosts; And all the nations will call you blessed, For you will be a delightful land, Says the LORD of hosts."
(Malachi 3:10-12)

"Give, and it will be given to you: good measure, pressed down, shaken together, and running over will be put into your bosom. For with the same measure that you use, it will be measured back to you."
(Luke 6:38)

"But this I say: He who sows sparingly will also reap sparingly, and he who sows bountifully will also reap bountifully. So let each one give as he purposes in his heart, not grudgingly or of necessity; for God loves a cheerful giver."
(2 Corinthians 9:6-7)

"And my God shall supply all your need according to His riches in glory by Christ Jesus."
(Philippians 4:19)

"Every good gift and every perfect gift is from above, and comes down from the Father of lights, with whom there is no variation or shadow of turning."
(James 1:17)

"Beloved, I pray that you may prosper in all things and be in health, just as your soul prospers."
(3 John 2)

Protection

"For He shall give His angels charge over you, To keep you in all your ways. In their hands they shall bear you up, Lest you dash your foot against a stone."
(Psalm 91:11-12)

"The name of the LORD is a strong tower; The righteous run to it, and are safe."
(Proverbs 18:10)

"So shall they fear The name of the LORD from the west, And His glory from the rising of the sun; When the enemy comes in like a flood, the Spirit of the LORD will lift up a standard against him."
(Isaiah 59:19)

"And who is he who will harm you if you become followers of what is good?"
(1 Peter 3:13)

"You are of God, little children, and have overcome them, because He who is in you is greater than he who is in the world."
(1 John 4:4)

Salvation

"But as many as received Him, to them He gave the right to become children of God, to those who believe in His name."
(John 1:12)

"For God so loved the world that He gave His only begotten Son, that whoever believes in Him should not perish but have everlasting life."
(John 3:16)

"But God demonstrates His own love toward us, in that while we were still sinners, Christ died for us."
(Romans 5:8)

"But what does it say? "The word is near you, in your mouth and in your heart" (that is, the word of faith which we preach): that if you confess with your mouth the Lord Jesus and believe in your heart that God has raised Him from the dead, you will be saved."
(Romans 10:8-9)

"For whoever calls on the name of the LORD shall be saved."
(Romans 10:13)

Sin

"For the wages of sin is death, but the gift of God is eternal life in Christ Jesus our Lord."
(Romans 6:23)

"Therefore, if anyone is in Christ, he is a new creation; old things have passed away; behold, all things have become new."
(2 Corinthians 5:17)

Strength

"He gives power to the weak, And to those who have no might He increases strength. Even the youths shall faint and be weary, And the young men shall utterly fall, But those who wait on the LORD Shall renew their strength; They shall mount up with wings like eagles, They shall run and not be weary, They shall walk and not faint."
(Isaiah 40:29-31)

Trials & Tribulations

"These things I have spoken to you, that in Me you may have peace. In the world you will have tribulation; but be of good cheer, I have overcome the world."
(John 16:33)

Wisdom

"The heart of the prudent acquires knowledge, And the ear of the wise seeks knowledge."
(Proverbs 18:15)

"If any of you lacks wisdom, let him ask of God, who gives to all liberally and without reproach, and it will be given to him."
(James 1:5)

Witnessing Bonus

Focus Scripture:

"For I am not ashamed of the gospel of Christ, for it is the power of God to salvation for everyone who believes, for the Jew first and also for the Greek." (Romans 1:16)

In social gatherings all over the world, people talk about drugs, sex, the news, their families, horrid lifestyles and so many other things, but when it comes to sharing Jesus with others, there seems to be a lot of dead air. It seems as though there is much shame and fear in some of us to share the "Good News" that Jesus is alive and well. Each time we fail to inform someone of the soon coming King, the devil is pleased that we have allowed him to win another victory.

Telemarketers call houses all day long to sell us the newest product on the market. What makes them so successful in their attempt to win us over? From my observation, I have found that they call us by our first names, as if they know us. They practice this procedure before they tell us what they are selling in order to soften our resistance. They are also prepared to tell us every reason why we should accept what they are offering. They do not take the first no for an answer and they are persistent with their pitch to push the product that they are promoting for whatever minuscule reward they might receive. We allow their diligence to trap us.

I have a serious concern with those of us who claim Christianity and are afraid to witness to others. As a Christian, we should be proactive in offering the greatest gift to those who may not know Jesus as their Savior. How can we become successful soul-winners for the kingdom? "My response" is that we should be prepared to tell others every reason why they should accept what we are offering. We cannot afford to take "no" for an answer because someone's soul may be lost. No matter what, do not give up! By offering Jesus to others, our reward will be great, *(Luke 6:23)*, and also, unlike the telemarketers thirty-day guarantee, salvation is FREE!

Salvation or Deliverance?

Blessings to you child of God! By the time you read this page, you should have either received salvation or deliverance, *if not, please refer to Chapter 9 on Salvation.*

If this book has led you to receive salvation, helped you to become free through the prayers of deliverance, or has ministered to you in anyway, we would love to hear from you. Please feel free to share your testimony with us about the wonderful things God has done for you.

We believe that you would perhaps find comfort to know that we will be praying for you and your continued deliverance as you strive to please the Lord in your daily walk.

To contact the author, write:

Dr. I. Franklin Perkins
P.O. Box 9523
Hampton, VA 23670
or view website

ItsmeDrIFP.org to order paperback books,
view itinerary or sow a seed.

Follow us on Twitter: @itsmedrifp

References

Scripture taken from the New King James
Version.
Copyright © 1979, 1980, 1982 by Thomas
Nelson, Inc.
Used by permission. All rights reserved.

King James Version
Copyright © 1994 by Thomas Nelson, Inc.
All Rights Reserved

Notes

Notes

Notes

_____

_____

_____

_____

_____

_____

_____

_____

_____

_____

_____

_____

_____

_____

About the Author

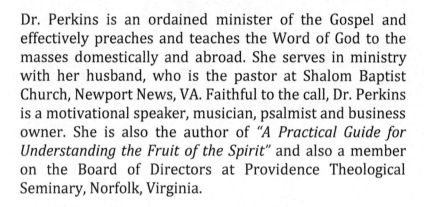

Dr. Perkins is an ordained minister of the Gospel and effectively preaches and teaches the Word of God to the masses domestically and abroad. She serves in ministry with her husband, who is the pastor at Shalom Baptist Church, Newport News, VA. Faithful to the call, Dr. Perkins is a motivational speaker, musician, psalmist and business owner. She is also the author of *"A Practical Guide for Understanding the Fruit of the Spirit"* and also a member on the Board of Directors at Providence Theological Seminary, Norfolk, Virginia.

She has academically prepared herself with: an ASB in Business Management, Penn Foster College, Scranton, PA; a BS in Business Administration and a MBA in Public Administration, Columbia Southern University, Orange Beach, AL; a MA in Practical Theology, Regent University, Virginia Beach, VA; a Doctorate in Ministry, United Theological Seminary, Dayton, OH; and currently working on a PhD in Management-Leadership and Organizational Change, Walden University, Minneapolis, MN. Dr. Perkins is also an instructor in the Gifts of the Holy Spirit, Christian International, Santa Rosa Beach; FL.

The author lives in Hampton, Virginia with her husband, their son and daughter.

Psalm 91:11-12

CPSIA information can be obtained at www.ICGtesting.com
Printed in the USA
BVOW08s0835181016

465148BV00004B/114/P